Five Principles of Green Witchcraft

Five Principles of Green Witchcraft

CC-BY-NC-SA 2020 Asa West
This work may be reproduced only for non-commercial reasons. All reproductions must bear attribution to the author and carry this identical license.

ISBN: 978-1-7325523-8-8
Reprinted with permission by
GODS&RADICALS PRESS

Cover Art by Asa West
Layout by Gods&Radicals Press

For bulk, solidarity, and wholesale copies
please contact us at
distro@abeautifulresistance.com

See our other books and online journal at
ABEAUTIFULRESISTANCE.ORG

"Do you think there is anything not attached by its unbreakable cord to everything else?" -Mary Oliver

Capitalism mechanizes all it touches, turning warm flesh and humming life into objects for production and consumption. Now it wants to sell us witchcraft, sanitized and stripped of power. We can no longer roam the untamed forests and live on the edge of the Otherworld; the land is maimed and owned, and our bodies and minds are poured into lifetimes of gratuitous labor in order to render us exhausted, pliant, and stupid. Thus robbed of our magic, we buy oils and crystals and jewelry that promise quick and shallow self-improvement—citrine for success, lavender for peace of mind—but these trinkets do not serve as allies in our magic. Rather, they serve as substitutes for it, so that we might never recognize the real thing. Under capitalism, everything is a commodity, and in the ideal capitalist landscape, all is burned, junked, and laid to waste, including the witchcraft we play at and then grow bored of. The drive for limitless wealth will not stop until it devours itself.

We may have been forcibly ripped from the land and its wordless, numinous song, but green witchcraft, operating on geologic time, survives. In our tamed and obedient imaginations, unable to conjure any image outside of materialism and consumption, the green witch has been reduced to a cheerful eccentric with a fondness for houseplants and essential oils, but green witchcraft is an immeasurably large and ancient thing, calling us to live in accordance with the deep laws of nature. Green witchcraft is a dedication to serving, understanding, and taking into oneself the living consciousness of the land. Green witchcraft is firmly animist, acknowledging the life and sentience of all nonhuman things. The green witch seeks to align herself with the rhythms of sacred ecology.

There are as many principles of green witchcraft as there are plant species in a biome, but perhaps these five can guide our practice as we seek to reenchant our devastated world.

Principle 1:
The Forest Speaks With One Voice

Consider the forest. Leaves and branches jostle for sunlight; tree roots mingle with mycorrhizal fungi while bacteria break bodies down into soil. Animals slink and forage and hunt and the air is a cacophony of birdsong. Each entity, removed from the forest, becomes self-contained and identifiable: the owl, the buck, the pine, the mushroom. Together, though, they create an entity larger than themselves: Forest.

The egregore, in occult lore, is the independent thoughtform that emerges from a focused group mind. The coven, each member in perfect alignment and intent on the spell being worked, creates an egregore. So do the ancestors of the deep past, individuals dissolving into a mass defined more by culture than by personality. The green witch offers themselves up to be absorbed into the egregore of the land around them, the host of spirits and beings that come together to give life to a place. No true green witch can believe herself alone on passive and unfeeling dirt; she cannot fall prey to destructive magic born of selfishness and self-aggrandizement; she cannot treat plant life and animal flesh as inert tools to be exploited. To work deep magic and strive toward the hidden light of wisdom, the witch must align his spirit and soul with the green.

One might envy the witches who live in wild, rural places; they are free to play and sing and weave spells with the august old-growth spirits. But the witch who lives and works in cities and suburbs is not cut off from the earth. The dandelion growing in a sidewalk crack is a member of the green witch's coven, as is the pigeon who pecks at the asphalt and the mouse who hides in the wall. If the witch's egregore is one of weeds and pests, so be it; the witch, too, is an outsider. The grand gods and the local gods, the devas and the Good Folk: the witch melts into their world to feed the egregore and perform its sacred work. Thus is the witch able to serve the land, hear its language, and speak with its voice.

Principle 2
Twilight Precedes Starlight

At the edge of tamed ground, the witch climbs a stile and lands topsy-turvy in the wilderness. The hedge-rider straddles this world and others so that he can slip between them. As night descends, twilight drapes the land with its eldritch half-light, a gossamer curtain that falls away to reveal the stars. There is a moment, each morning and evening, when one truly cannot say whether it is day or night, when familiar categories fall away and order is lost. These moments are potent. The liminal is a sacred place.

The crossroads. The magic circle. The invocation. The trance journey. To work magic, the witch uses these arts to travel to a place like the boundary between two ecosystems, in which unique species thrive in the richness of the border. In-between places, places that are not-quite-this and not-quite-that, hold infinite paths and possibilities. The timberline guards the hidden groves; the frog on the lakeshore watches the Otherworld; the sea slowly whittles caves into the cliffside. At dawn and dusk and cross-quarter days, day is night and winter is spring and the world slips and tumbles from our attempts to define it. Magic lives everywhere, but in the liminal places, which confound the senses and blunt the rational mind, the green witch can most easily touch it. When the witch weaves their magic in twilight, they open themselves to starlight vision: the ability to perceive that which is occluded, just as the stars are revealed by the absence of the sun. Indeed, the witch's gods themselves are liminal beings: human figures with horns and antlers and the heads of animals, fertility goddesses who govern war and death, guardians of the crossroads and keepers of hidden light.

To seek that light, the witch descends into the murk of soil and swamp; he faces demons and monsters to find their hidden beauty. All is in flux and change is constant; in truth, all is liminal. But this truth is hidden in our safe and comfortable places, the places in which our senses lie to us, saying, "yes, all is as it seems; there are no surprises here." The green witch knows that the journey through twilight into the dazzle of starlight cannot be hurried or discarded. She knows she must approach the ancient spirits mindfully, with awe and reverence and attention, in order to cross these borderlands. Then, in order to bring back knowledge and act upon it, he must ride the hedge to return to the civilized world, reluctant though he may be to leave the starlight behind.

If the green witch seeks liminal places in time and space and within their own mind, barriers to their magic will fall away. If they seek the liminal and recognize it within the mundane, they will fall upon the deepest wisdom of all: that within the churning cauldron of birth and death and change, all is unified and all is one.

Principle 3
Witchcraft Lives in the Body

It is known that we each have three selves: the conscious self, the primal self, and the divine self. These selves are the Triple Soul of Feri witchcraft and the Talking, Child, and Deep selves of the Reclaiming tradition; they are known by many names. Witchcraft lives beneath the conscious self, in the place where instinct and intuition produce dreams and visions. The green witch's conscious self cannot initiate witchcraft and magic. It can only create the right conditions for her animal self to bring it forth. The witch creates these conditions through sound, movement, and intoxication: the beat of a drum, the whirring of a bullroarer, the dizzying movement of dance, the intonation of chants and vowel sounds, and the ingesting of sacred plants—many of which lie on the razor's edge between ally and poison, daring the witch to teeter at the edge of death and return. The conscious self shouts down the insights of the body, ridiculing the sacred and stamping out the ecstasies of magic. It is through somatic means that the witch invites twilight to mute the relentless chatter of the rational mind.

Once the primal self is awakened, the body of the earth will speak directly to the body of the witch. It sparks in his brainstem and stirs memories of when he was soil and bacteria and plant life and animal flesh, before he coalesced into his own separate human body. Through the language of the earth, the witch grows horns and wings and claws, hearing the voices of the spirits who flock to her as they paw and scratch and kiss and caress, eager to join her coven. She remembers the future, when her body will dissipate into the ecosystem once again. The witch travels to the beginning of cellular metabolism, the birth of the first microscopic ancestor, and then further to the explosion of the stars and dust that formed her.

Many witches speak of virtue, the serpent-power that flows through the arteries of the earth and animates all things. This is the power the green witch accesses and gathers when they learn to enter twilight and open the channels of their body, and it is by raising and directing this power through those channels that the witch works magic. Thus does the green witch become a limb of the breathing earth and the living cosmos. This is where green witchcraft lives: in the great body that encompasses us all.

Principle 4
The Witch Always Pays Her Coin

In the leaf of a plant, the chloroplast takes water, air, and sunlight and uses them to make sugars. The sugars, in turn, feed growing buds that unfurl into new leaves. The plant's growth looks, on the outside, like a miracle: leaves from nowhere, matter from nothing.

But matter cannot come from nothing, and every prize has a price. Matter continuously cycles through ecosystems, eternally in motion and eternally transformed, and it cannot disappear or be hoarded. Plants and creatures work for their food; energy flows and bottlenecks of power are always flushed out. A would-be witch's casual desire for magic will not bring forth magic, and a half-hearted wish will not open one's eyes to the spirit world. Instead, the witch must work, with discipline and devotion and respect, to reach twilight and raise power. She studies, she sings, she attunes herself to the earth and enters its ancient rhythms. He coaxes virtue from the land and uses it to actualize his will; then he tends to the land and serves it and thus replenishes its power. The witch leaves candies and coins and bowls of milk for the spirits they work with not because those spirits demand sacrifice, but because vacuums will always be filled. The green witch knows that will without reciprocity is abuse, and magic will collect its payment one way or another. Why not pay the coin in partnership and on one's own terms, instead of waiting for the egregore to take it in some unpredictable way?

The witch must take care not to exploit, lest she suffer the backlash, but so must the gods and spirits. How many cults have disappeared because their gods grew greedy and vain? How many spiritual seekers have left their gods to regain lost dignity and freedom, and found their former masters suddenly powerless to stop them? When a thing is taken, something else must be given; when a thing is given, something else must be taken. The green witch must not fall prey to slavish devotion and dogma. She knows that her human mind and body are as holy as the gods and the land, and she works alongside them accordingly. The witch venerates all life and is subservient to none, and thus is balance maintained.

Principle 5
The Goddess Reveals Herself in Silence

We have been taught to obliterate silence at all costs, filling periods of stillness with extra work or frantic amusement, or else to be silent in the service of oppressors, guarding the secrets of rapists and abusers, gagging ourselves to keep from speaking out against tyrants. Most humans under capitalism have never encountered true sacred silence.

But silence is where power resides. When we resist our own capacity for silence, we let our power leak away. When we unwillingly keep silence for others, we give our power to them. Those who abide by the Witch's Pyramid—to know, to will, to dare, and to keep silent—know that silence keeps the power of a spell contained as it is focused and directed, keeping pressure on its magic like the lid of a kettle on to boil.

But the fourth corner of the Witch's Pyramid has another purpose as well. Boasting to the world that you have worked a spell depletes that spell's power, it is true. But the practice of silence is deeper than simply not talking. When the witch cultivates silence in their mind, quieting thoughts and chatter, stilling hopes and expectations, they also cultivate the ability to recognize the fruits of their magic. What a pity when a spell brings great rewards in an unexpected way, but the witch is too distracted to see them!

This ability to notice—to listen, see, and observe without expectation or prejudice—is one of the green witch's most fundamental skills. Just as everything is alive, so does everything have its place in the egregore's song, and so the green witch listens, and hears the spirits calling her true name. The spirits are calling; they call incessantly; they wait and wait for the sleeping witch to awaken and answer. The green witch howls and drums and sings and chants and lets the beauty of incantation roll on his tongue; then he lets his voice fade and fall silent to create a gateway for wisdom. She listens for the languages of the birds and trees and rivers. She knows that the voices of the most ancient gods speak in whispers. She practices the art of hearing the silence underneath the egregore, of following that silence to find the hidden light in the darkness.

When the burgeoning green witch feels they are ready to undertake a practice informed by these principles, and when they are driven by their desire to serve and embody the land, they shall make a pilgrimage at twilight to a wild and lonely place, whether it is far in the wilderness or nestled within an overgrown and forgotten corner of a city. So much the better if the moon is full, or if the morning or evening star is visible, or if the day is a Sabbat or other holy day—but the witch shall not fret over perfection. Rather, she shall go when her body urges her to do so, for her body listens to the call of the spirits.

When the witch arrives, he shall first banish malicious influences using the tools to which he is accustomed. The witch shall then demark ritual space through the building of a simple altar or the creation of a circle or compass, according to the practices of his tradition. When the space is marked, the witch shall enter it and cultivate a twilight trance. She might whip a bullroarer around her head to delight the spirits and invite their aid. She might drum rhythmically or chant io evoe, words that invoke Isis and Dionysus— mother of all and god of spiritual ecstasy—and, by requiring the steady outflow of breath, encourage virtue to move from the earth upward through the body. The witch shall continue to cultivate trance until an altered state is achieved, when the gathering dusk appears sharper and brighter, when the mind is stilled and focused, when spirits can perhaps be seen and heard out of the corner of the eye. The witch must not rush this phase of the ritual. If the cultivation of trance takes an hour or an entire night, so be it.

When trance is achieved, the witch shall then greet the spirits of the wild place: the genius loci, the Good Folk, and the guardian spirits of the place's plants and creatures. If the witch is on colonized land, they shall humbly greet the spirits of its Indigenous ancestors. The witch shall then conjure her patron deities, ancestors, familiars, and guides, welcoming them and asking for their blessings.

The witch shall then state her intention to those assembled: to hear the voices of the land and the spirit world, so that she may serve as an ally and partner to them. Then the witch shall fall silent, and listen.

This ritual is at once the simplest and most difficult act the witch will perform. He must be aware of the chatter in his mind, chatter that will relentlessly tug at his thoughts on subtler and subtler levels, so that even when he believes he has succeeded in quieting his mind, it continues to be jerked this way and that like a terrier on a leash. He must be aware of the false messages conjured by his ego, voices that will take the shape of gods in order to lure him into self-aggrandizement. He must be aware of the apparitions caused by wishful thinking and impatience, creating the specters of spirits where there are none so that he may carry a supposedly mystical experience away with him like a bead on a gaudy necklace.

After spending some time listening earnestly, with discipline and patience, the witch may hear the voice of the egregore or see one of its manifestations. This sign might take the form of a bird call or animal, or perhaps a gust of wind, or a sudden knowing. The witch may, if she finds it useful, follow her period of listening with a period of divination with tools like cards or bones, asking the egregore to converse in the language to which she is accustomed. If the witch does not hear the egregore during her first ritual, she shall repeat it regularly, with faith and goodwill.

When the ritual is complete, the witch shall offer food and drink to the spirits, deities, ancestors, and guides she invoked, regardless of whether she felt their presence. She shall then return again and again, performing the work of a lifetime.

I am grateful for the writings and teachings of Peter Grey, Gemma Gary, Robin Wall Kimmerer, Starhawk, Karina BlackHeart, and Griffin Ced, whose work informed these principles.

Further reading

Apocalyptic Witchcraft by Peter Grey

A Witch's Book of Silence by Karina BlackHeart

Braiding Sweetgrass by Robin Wall Kimmerer

Spiritual Ecology edited by Llewellyn Vaughan-Lee

The Earth Path and *The Spiral Dance* by Starhawk

Traditional Witchcraft by Gemma Gary

This essay was first published, in different form, in *Venefica*, Vol/Issue 3, published by Catland Books, LLC.

ASA WEST

Asa West practices and teaches traditional witchcraft in Los Angeles, California.

You can find her at tarotbyasa.com and on Instagram at @TheRedTailWitch.

GODS&RADICALS PRESS

is a non-profit pagan anti-capitalist publisher founded on Beltane, 2015.

This is our 19th publication. To see our other books, please visit

ABEAUTIFULRESISTANCE.ORG

www.ingramcontent.com/pod-product-compliance
Lightning Source LLC
Chambersburg PA
CBHW071326080526
44587CB00018B/3357